KT-546-936

Nail Art Studio

**Lorna Davidson, Heather Hammonds
and Jaclyn Crupi**

hinkler

About This Book

This book will show you everything you need to know to transform your fingernails and toenails into works of art.

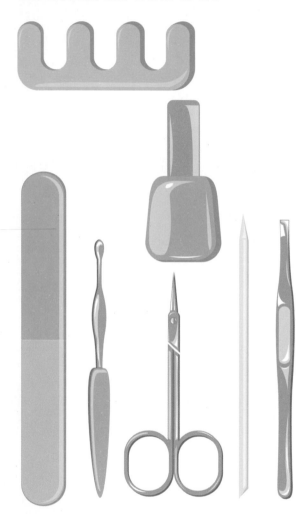

For perfect nails you will need:
· Nail art stickers
· Nail gems
· Nail file
· Toe separators
· Nail polish
· Nail scissors
· Striping tape
· Dotting tools
· Nail sponges
· Geometric stickers
· Hoof stick or orange stick
· Nail art pen
· Nail polish remover
· Base coat
· Top coat
· Buffer block
· Hand and feet moisturiser

Images © Shutterstock.com: Girls painting their toes © Michelle D. Milliman; Nail art accessories © oxanaart; Coloured false nail shapes © De-V; Hands with henna art on them © Olena Zaskochenko; Hands held together with bright fingernails © bezikus; Two hands with colourful nails © Hakan Kiziltan; Fingernail diagram © Grei; Nail file, Cuticle cream © Valua Vitaly; Orange stick, Nail Scissors © AISPIX by Image Source; Buffer block, Painting toes with red nail polish © wavebreakmedia; Toe separators © Serg Zastavkin; Cherries © Valentyn Volkov; Bottle of milk and cheese © Rafa Irusta; Fish © Jiang Hongyan; Fresh fruit and vegetables © Evgenia Sc.; Washing hands © 3445128471; Hands putting on hand cream © Olga Miltsova; Child with hat, scarf and gloves on © Tuboi Evgeniya; Putting on clear nail polish © Serghei Starus; Two nail files © Cristi 180884; Nails with a bottle of hand cream © Dr. Cloud; Sprigs of lavender © Scisetti Alfio; Girl with hands spread (cover), Pink nail varnish, Red glittery nail polish, Fingers showing, holding spilling polish © Africa Studio; Pots of coloured glitter © Ruzanna; Girl in shades with coloured nails © Elegor; Hands painting top coat on black nails © Dean Bertoncelj; Hands/nail design © Teddy2007b; Sticking gems on nails from a pot, Closer up images of sticking gems on nails © pzAxe; Young girl painting pink nails © GWImages; Close up image of girl painting red nails © Elena Rostunova; Taking off nail varnish with cotton wool © Dusan Jankovic; Girl painting nails © Christo; Pink glossy nails © bezikus; Spilt glittery nail polish © Alexandra Lande; Top of pot and a dipping brush © pogonici; Shattered black image © New Line; Four pots of spilling nail polish © Foonia; Waves on a beach © Imagevixen; Slices of watermelon © panda3800; Rainbow © Jaroslav Bartoš; Penguin © javarman; Smiling girl painting her nails © 41; Toes/feet © kittasgraphics; Toes in holiday flip flops © Cheryl Casey; Girl painting toes © Duard van der Westhuizen; Girl painting her toes in her pyjamas © Aspen Photo; Pedicure items © Amalia Ferreira-Espinoza; Sparkly pink flip flops © S.A.S. Photography; Thumb massaging foot © Hywit Dimyadi; Fist massaging heel © vita khorzhevska; Two hands massaging foot © VILevi; Two fingers massaging foot © Yuri Arcurs; Leopard © LauraDyer; Lightning © italianphoto; Geometric pattern © Fedorov Oleksiy; Reindeer © Wolfgang Kruck; Easter eggs © leungchopan; Red graphic heart © art@design.

Contents

Nail Art Origins

Many people think that painting and decorating fingernails and toenails is a recent trend. So it might come as a surprise to learn that nail art is about 7000 years old! In 5000 BCE Indian women began to dye their fingertips with henna – a practice that still continues.

In 3000 BCE the Chinese began to use enamel on their nails. They applied a mixture of gum arabic (acacia gum), gelatin, beeswax, vegetable dyes and egg whites and left it on their nails for several hours and sometimes even overnight. The result was a pink finish on their nails. This was the beginning of nail art.

Nail art also has origins in Egypt. The shade of Egyptian ladies' nails was used to identify what class in society they were in. The higher class used deep shades of red and lower classes wore pale shades. The Inca civilisation also used nail art – they painted images of eagles on their fingertips.

Modern manicures began in Europe in about 1830. The trend spread to the USA by the late 19th century. The next milestone to happen to nail art actually had nothing to do with nails. A new range of paints became available thanks to the automobile industry. The range of colours suddenly available made nail art more popular than ever.

Today, nail art is more detailed and exciting than ever before. The only limit is your imagination!

Nail File

The first bottle of Revlon nail polish hit the shelves in 1932 in colours never seen before.

Nails Today

Nails have become part of the whole outfit, with nail art stickers providing a never-before-achieved level of intricacy to manicure designs.

Nail Art Timeline

5000 BCE
Indian women dye their hands and nails with henna.

3000 BCE
The Chinese use an enamel to colour their nails.

600 BCE
Aristocrats in China begin to wear gold or silver bejewelled nail guards.

1400s
The Incas decorate their nails with detailed pictures of eagles.

1830s
Women in Europe begin to manicure their nails.

1930s
Revlon's nail polish hits stores in a range of colours. The first set of fake nails is created.

1920s
Women paint their nails bright colours and with moon shapes.

1980s
Bright neon colours become popular.

2010s
Adhesives mean nails can be more detailed than ever before. Shellac becomes popular. DIY nail art is limited only by imagination.

All About Nails

Before we get stuck into finding out ways to make our nails look great we need to know a bit about them.

Your fingernails and toenails are made of a tough protein called keratin. This same substance is found in animal claws, feathers and fur. In humans, nails grow at an average rate of 3 mm (0.12 inches) per month. They grow faster in the summer than in any other season.

We have nails to protect our fingertips and toes from injuries. They also help our fingers and toes to move and make our fingertips and toes more sensitive. And, of course, with the addition of nail art they look fabulous.

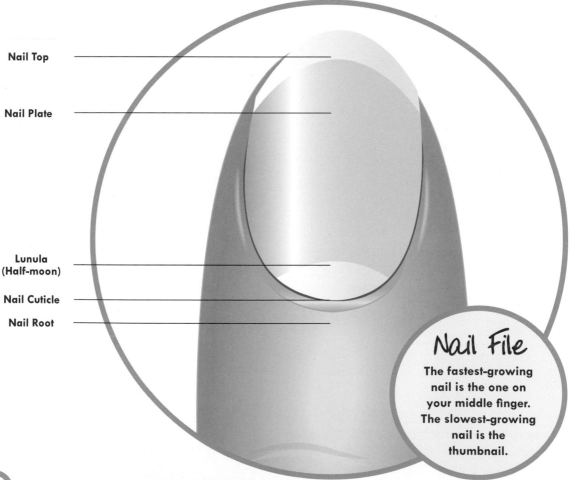

Nail Top

Nail Plate

Lunula (Half-moon)

Nail Cuticle

Nail Root

Nail File

The fastest-growing nail is the one on your middle finger. The slowest-growing nail is the thumbnail.

Tools of the Trade

ALL NAIL ARTISTS NEED BASIC TOOLS

Nail Files

There are different types of nail files. Some have coarse surfaces and others are finer. Emery boards have a coarse surface and are used to shorten nails quickly whilst shaping them. Nail files with a fine surface are used to file a small amount of nail.

Hoof Sticks/Orange Sticks

Hoof sticks and orange sticks are used to gently push back your cuticles from the base of the nail.

Buffer Block

Buffing helps your nails to grow as it increases the flow of blood in the nail bed. Buffing also takes off the dull top layers of the nail and builds up shine. This leaves a smooth surface ready for polish.

Nail Scissors

Nail scissors have slightly curved short blades. They are very sharp, so be careful. Nail scissors are used mainly to cut the length of a nail and the shaping is done with a file.

Cuticle Cream/Oil

There is a variety of cuticle treatments available and they are used to soften the cuticle (the skin at the base of the nail).

Toe Separators

Placed between the toes, toe separators make painting toenails much easier. Leave them on until toenails are dry.

Nail Care

Making your nails look great with nail art is one thing, but they need to be healthy and in good condition first. The health of your nails is affected by two main factors:
- **What you eat and drink.**
- **How you care for your nails.**

FOOD AND WATER

To make sure your nails are healthy you need to eat a well-balanced diet and drink plenty of water. Nails need protein, vitamins and minerals to grow.

- Vitamin A helps nails grow and is found in green vegetables, carrots, tomatoes, apricots and cherries.

- Calcium is important for the strength of your nails and is found in fish and dairy products such as milk, yoghurt and cheese.

- Iodine also helps nails grow and is found in fish, spinach and watercress.

- Sulphur is essential for nail consistency and is found in cabbage, onions and cucumbers.

CARING FOR YOUR NAILS

Moisture is essential to keep your nails strong and flexible so that they do not become dry, flake or break easily. The best ways to keep your nails moist and protected are:

After washing your hands and feet be sure to dry your nails well, this stops them from drying out.

Massage cuticle cream, baby oil, massage oil or olive oil around your cuticles (the skin at the base of the nail).
Use a cotton wool bud soaked in olive oil to push cuticles back from the nail.

Wear gloves in cold weather and rubber gloves when washing up, gardening or cleaning.

When not wearing polish or nail art stickers apply a clear varnish or protective nail strengthener to your nails.

File and buff your nails regularly.

Mani Madness

MANICURE STEPS

Manicures are an important step in caring for your nails. They moisturise, shape and prepare your nails for the fun part of painting them or applying nail art stickers.

1 Soak your fingers in a bowl of warm water for about two minutes.

2 Use a towel to dry each nail.

3 Gently push back the cuticles (the skin around the base of the fingernail) from the nail with a cotton bud soaked in olive oil or a hoof or orange stick.

4 Using a buffer block, buff the nail surface to remove the dull top nail cell layers.

5 Massage baby oil, olive oil or cuticle oil into the cuticle and surrounding skin of each nail. This moisturises each cuticle thoroughly and also stimulates blood circulation in the nail bed.

6 Dry hands thoroughly.

7 Trim nails to the desired length with nail scissors.

8 File nails into the desired shape. File from the side to the centre of the nail, holding the nail file at an angle. Never file back and forth as this may cause flaking and splitting. For a squared-off look, file nails straight across the top. For a round finish, file the nail down a little on each side and round across the top of the nail.

9 As an extra treat you can give yourself a relaxing hand massage.

HAND MASSAGE

As well as relaxing your hands, a hand massage improves blood flow to your nails. You should not massage your hands if you suffer from painful, swollen joints or fingers. You will need massage oil or hand cream.

1 Relax and loosen each wrist by rotating it gently around.

2 Pour a little oil or hand cream into the palm of one hand and gently rub all over your hands and nails.

3 Using your thumb, massage the back of each hand and knuckle using a firm backward motion.

4 Massage each finger, one at a time.

5 Extend the massage to the wrist and lower arm.

Top Tip

Add a few drops of fragrant essential oil (lavender or rose for example) to your massage oil for a relaxing aromatherapy massage.

Fantastic Fingers

Now that you know about nails and nail care in general let's focus on making your nails look fantastic. It's super fun and it can be so simple to create amazing nails. Soon all your family and friends will want to know how you did it.

There are lots of things you can use to decorate your nails and make them look cool and fabulous.

Nail Art Stickers

Nail art stickers are fun and easy to apply (see pages 14 to 15). Nail art stickers are not permanent. They stick to your real nails and actually protect them.

Nail Polish

Nail polish can be applied as a simple single colour or used to create intricate designs and pictures. There really is no limit to what you can do. Pages 24 to 29 will show you with step-by-step instructions how to create some cool nail polish designs.

Glitter Sparkle

You can buy glittery nail polish. An even simpler way to get a glittery finish is to apply a clear coat of nail polish and then dip your fingers into a pot of super-fine glitter.

Nail Gems

Nail gems come in all shapes and sizes. They are a quick and easy way to make your nails bling. They can be glued on and used to jazz up a simple base colour or incorporated in a more complicated design.

Striping Tape

Striping tape allows you to add lines to a design quickly and with precision. You simply cut the amount of tape that you need and lay it across your nail, letting it overhang your nail on both ends, and paint over it. Then remove once dry!

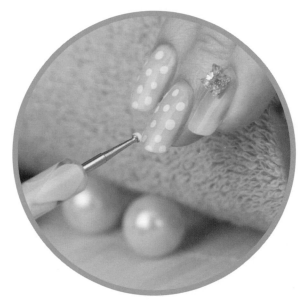

Dotting Tools

Dotting tools make forming dots on your nails easy. Simply dip the tool into your nail polish of choice and apply dots to your nails, dipping the tool into more polish as needed. Dotting tools come in different sizes allowing you to achieve dots of the perfect size every time.

Nail Sponges

Nail sponges help in an ombre (or gradient) effect. Paint stripes of the polish colours of your choice onto a sponge about the size of your largest nail, being generous with the liquid. Then take the painted edge and sponge it onto your nail. Pat it a few times and you move it up and down slightly. Voila!

Removable Stickers

Removable stickers are used to cover parts of your nail while you paint. You could paint your nail one colour and then place a semi-circle sticker at the base of your nail and paint the nail a contrasting colour. Once done, you pull the sticker off to show through to the layer below.

Nail Art Stickers

HOW TO APPLY NAIL ART STICKERS

Nail art stickers are not permanent and are easily applied; they stick to your real nails.

1 Prepare your nails by buffing them. This helps to make the nail stickers easier to stick on. Ideally follow the steps on pages 10 to 11 and give yourself a full manicure before you start.

2 Apply a clear nail varnish. Because your nails produce their own natural oils, nail stickers won't stick well unless nails are varnished.

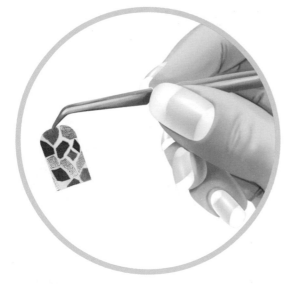

3 Lift your chosen nail stickers from their backing sheet with tweezers.

4 Line up the nail sticker with your cuticle and place it gently on your nail. When you are happy with the position, pat down gently using a hoof or orange stick. You could also use a dotting tool to do this.

5 Trim or file the nail sticker as needed to fit your fingernail shape.

6 Protect your nail stickers by applying a layer of top coat.

Nail Sticker Removal

Wash hands in warm soapy water and gently peel off nail art stickers.

Top Tip

When doing your own nails, make sure that you take your nail stickers out of their packet and have a hoof or orange stick and tweezers on hand before you put your top coat on — that way you won't smudge your polish when taking them out of the pack.

Mix It Up

When looking at all your nail art stickers, don't feel you have to use the same design on each finger. It's fun to mix things up.

Not every nail needs to look the same. In fact, to create a memorable effect it would look great to use nail polish on each alternate finger and some of the stickers or striping tape on the other fingers. You could also use glitter on some nails – not to mention adding gems for effect.

It's best to plan out your nail design creations before you start. Use the hand outlines on these pages to draw out your designs and make creative decisions before you get started.

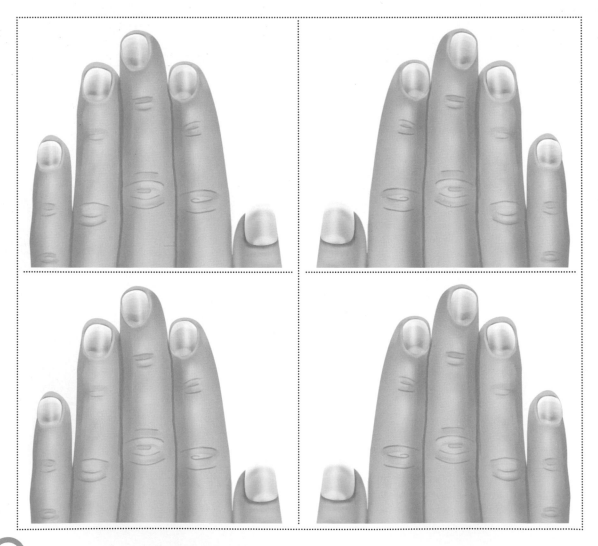

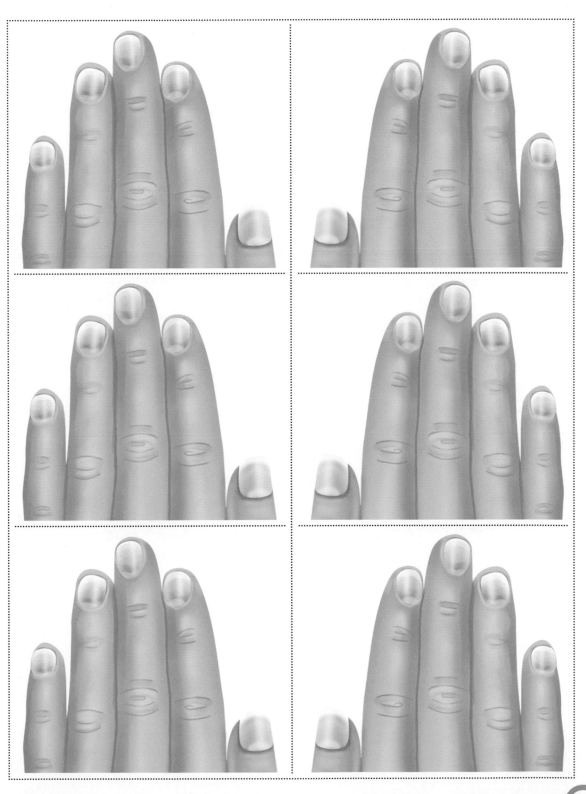

HOW TO APPLY NAIL GEMS

Gems add a bit of sparkle and shine to any nail design. They can be used on their own or in conjunction with polish, nail art stickers or glitter.

1 Prepare your nails by buffing them. Ideally follow the steps on pages 10 to 11 and give yourself a full manicure before you start.

2 Apply a base coat to your nails.

3 Choose a nail polish colour that complements the gem colours you have chosen and apply two coats. Allow the polish to dry thoroughly.

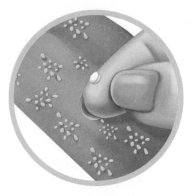

4 Carefully peel off the protective backing from the gem.

5 Using tweezers, position the gem on your nail. Press firmly in place for several seconds.

6 Apply a top coat to protect both your polish and gem.

Top Tip

You can buy nail glue from most beauty stores. Use it to re-affix any gems that fall off. It can also be used to secure the ends of striping tape if they peel.

TOUGH OR GIRLY

Depending on your design choices you can use gems to make your nails look girly or more edgy. A pastel base colour topped with colourful gems will give a girly look while a black polish base topped with silver studs will make a more edgy impression.

STRAIGHT OR SCATTERED

How you choose to apply the gems will also affect the look of your nails. The gems can be placed in straight rows on each nail (three rows of three gems for example) or more randomly for a fun look.

Nail Polish

HOW TO APPLY A SINGLE COLOUR

Using nail polish to create nail art allows you to achieve the most unique results. But it's also the most difficult to perfect and takes lots of practice. Don't be disheartened though; working with nail polish is loads of fun.

1 Prepare your nails by buffing them. This helps to prepare your nails for polish. Ideally follow the steps on pages 10 to 11 and give yourself a full manicure before you start.

2 Apply a layer of base coat. Try to keep the base coat away from the cuticles as it has a drying effect on them. Allow to dry.

3 Apply a thin layer of your chosen nail polish colour. Paint each nail with three strokes. Start the first stroke down the centre of the nail followed by one stroke on either side of it. Allow to dry.

4 If you get any nail polish on the skin surrounding your fingernails, dip a cotton wool bud in a little nail polish remover and remove polish carefully.

5 Apply a second coat of your chosen nail polish colour. Use the same technique as the first coat. It's always best to apply two coats if you can.

6 Apply a top coat to give your nails a glossy, professionally manicured look. Allow your nails to dry for about half an hour. Try not to bump your nails as it's easy to smudge the polish at this stage.

HOW TO REMOVE NAIL POLISH

1 Soak cotton wool in nail polish remover.

2 Press the cotton wool onto your nail for a few seconds, then wipe off the nail polish.

3 If you are not using an acetone-free remover, apply baby oil to your cuticles to protect them from drying out.

Salvaging Smudges

Dip your finger in some nail polish remover and rub it over the smudged area of the nail. Take your nail polish colour and go back over the area. Apply a top coat to smooth everything over. Simple!

Types of Nail Polish

There is a huge variety of nail polishes available, from neon to glitter to shatter. They each give a different look and feel to your nails so you can create any design that you're trying to achieve.

Gloss/Creme

Gloss/creme polishes are pure colours and have a great shine and smoothness to them.

Glitter

Glitter polishes are usually clear polish with tiny bits of glitter mixed in. You can apply a colour base and then the glitter polish on top for a change.

Matte

Matte polishes have no shine to them. Do not use a base coat or top coat with matte polishes.

Metallic

Metallic polishes usually contain a gold or silver shimmer, which adds a depth to the colour.

Shatter

Shatter polishes give a crackled texture to your nails as they dry. Try them for something different.

Polish Design

There's more to nail polish than single-colour applications. Once you have mastered the basics it's time to take your nails to a whole new level.

The next six pages will show you in simple steps how to create some unique nail art designs using nail polish. Use this page to plan your own designs. Don't be afraid to mix things up!

Spots and Stripes

HOW TO APPLY SPOTS AND STRIPES

Spots and stripes are two simple designs you can apply to your coloured nails. They add a fun twist and you can use any colour combination you like. You could also alternate spots and stripes.

1 Start by buffing your nails. This helps to prepare your nails for polish. Ideally follow the steps on pages 10 to 11 and give yourself a full manicure before you start.

2 Follow the instructions on page 20 to apply a single colour but stop before you put on the top coat.

3 Using a dotting tool, gently place small dots on each nail. If you don't have a dotting tool you can use a fine nail brush or even a toothpick. For stripes, use a dotting tool and gently draw straight lines on each nail.

4 Apply a top coat to give your nails a glossy, professionally manicured look. Allow your nails to dry for about half an hour. Try not to bump your nails as it's easy to smudge the polish at this stage.

Top Tip

Play with the size of the spots you paint on your fingers. Small dots look really cute; large dots are playful and fun. Dotting tools come in a range of sizes and allow you to paint different-sized perfect dots on your nails.

Stripe Lines

HOW TO APPLY STRIPE LINES

Stripe lines are a fun design that will draw lots of attention to your nails. Be sure to use contrasting and playful colour combinations.

1 Start by buffing your nails. This helps to prepare your nails for polish. Ideally follow the steps on pages 10 to 11 and give yourself a full manicure before you start.

2 Follow the instructions on page 20 to apply a single colour but stop before you put on the top coat.

3 Apply striping tape to each nail in different patterns. Make sure the tape is longer than your nails so it's easier to peel off.

4 Apply a single coat of a contrasting colour to the base colour.

5 Carefully pull off the strips of striping tape.

6 Apply a top coat to give your nails a glossy, professionally manicured look. Allow your nails to dry for about half an hour. Try not to bump your nails as it's easy to smudge the polish at this stage.

Top Tip

Remember, the slower you remove the striping tape, the less likely that it will disrupt your beautiful nail polish.

Ombres

HOW TO APPLY OMBRES

Sponges allow you to easily create an ombre effect.

1 Start by buffing your nails. This helps to prepare your nails for polish. Ideally follow the steps on pages 10 to 11 and give yourself a full manicure before you start.

2 Cut your sponge so you have a flat edge that's roughly the same size as your largest nail.

3 Apply stripes of nail polish (you can use two to five colours) to the sponge edge. Be generous with the amount of polish you apply.

4 Dab the sponge onto each nail, ensuring that it covers the width of the nail, moving it up and down slightly. Apply more polish to the sponge as needed.

5 Use nail polish remover to remove any polish on your fingers.

6 Apply a top coat to give your nails a glossy, professionally manicured look. Allow your nails to dry for about half an hour. Try not to bump your nails as it's easy to smudge the polish at this stage.

Top Tip

You can use contrasting colours when creating ombre nails or similar colours. Similar colours have a more subtle gradient effect.

Watermelons

HOW TO APPLY WATERMELON NAILS

There is nothing cuter than watermelons painted on your nails. This sweet design will have your friends wanting to know how you did it.

1 Prepare your nails by buffing them. This design works best on square nails. Ideally follow the steps on pages 10 to 11 and give yourself a full manicure before you start.

2 Follow the instructions on page 20 to apply a single colour (use hot pink polish) but stop before you put on the top coat.

3 Apply a thick line of green polish along the tip of your nail.

4 Add up to five black dots in an arc on the pink part of your nail. Try to make them teardrop-shaped.

5 Paint squiggly white or light green lines on the green tip.

6 Apply a top coat to give your nails a glossy, professionally manicured look and protect your watermelon creations. Allow your nails to dry for about half an hour. Try not to bump your nails as it's easy to smudge the polish at this stage.

Top Tip

The black seeds don't have to be in an arc. You could paint them randomly if you want. Or leave them out entirely if you prefer seedless watermelon!

Rainbows

HOW TO APPLY RAINBOW NAILS

Rainbow-tipped nails look bright and cheery. They are sure to brighten any rainy day.

1 Prepare your nails by buffing them. This design works best on squared-off nails. Ideally follow the steps on pages 10 to 11 and give yourself a full manicure before you start.

2 Follow the instructions on page 20 to apply a single colour (use a transparent glitter polish) but stop before you put on the top coat.

3 Paint a blue arc across the nail.

4 Once it's dry, paint a yellow arc and then a red one.

5 Apply overlapping thick white dots on the fingernail tip for clouds.

6 Apply a top coat to give your nails a glossy, professionally manicured look and protect your rainbow creations. Allow your nails to dry for about half an hour. Try not to bump your nails as it's easy to smudge the polish at this stage.

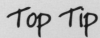

Top Tip

When you're doing the stripes for the rainbow, get a good amount of paint on your brush and apply it nice and slowly to avoid streaking.

Penguins

HOW TO APPLY PENGUIN NAILS

Penguins are adorable. Penguin nail art is even more adorable!

1 Prepare your nails by buffing them. This design works best on squared-off nails. Ideally follow the steps on pages 10 to 11 and give yourself a full manicure before you start.

2 Follow the instructions on page 20 to apply a single colour (use a light blue polish) but stop before you put on the top coat.

3 Apply a white oval from the tip of the nail to three quarters down. Leave a bit of blue on either side and some at the base.

4 Use a dotting tool to dot two black eyes.

5 Use a nail art pen or dotting tool to add two orange feet to the tip of the nail.

6 Use a nail art pen to add an orange dot for the beak and gently drag the polish down to make a triangle shape.

7 Apply a top coat to give your nails a glossy, professionally manicured look and protect your penguin creations. Allow your nails to dry, ideally for about half an hour. Try not to bump your nails as it's easy to smudge the polish at this stage.

Top Tip

The base colour doesn't have to be blue. Try any bright colour for a cute, cartoon-inspired look.

Nail It

Creating nail art can be heaps of fun. It requires lots of patience though, and trial and error. Never be deterred – one of the great things about nail art is that it's not permanent and you can always take it off and start again!

Make sure you always think about colour combinations as well as overall design. Don't be afraid to experiment and try new things. Nails are a fun way to express your creativity and artistic abilities.

It's often easier to do someone else's nails than your own, so get some friends together and experiment with nail art as a group.

This book has shown some design options but there are plenty more, plus some that don't even exist yet – you need to create them!

Toe-rrific

Because our toes spend so much time in shoes it's easy to forget about them. But the nail art possibilities that exist for our fingernails can also be explored for our toes. Every day we walk, run and stand on our feet for hours. They deserve our attention.

Summertime and parties are the time when beautiful feet and toenails really come into their own. Whether you're wearing sandals or flip-flops, or just walking barefoot on the beach, sparkling toenails are sure to catch everyone's attention.

So where can you get some great tips to brighten up your tootsies? Right here! The following pages contain heaps of information on how to care for your feet and toes. You'll also be inspired by the nail art possibilities for your terrific toes.

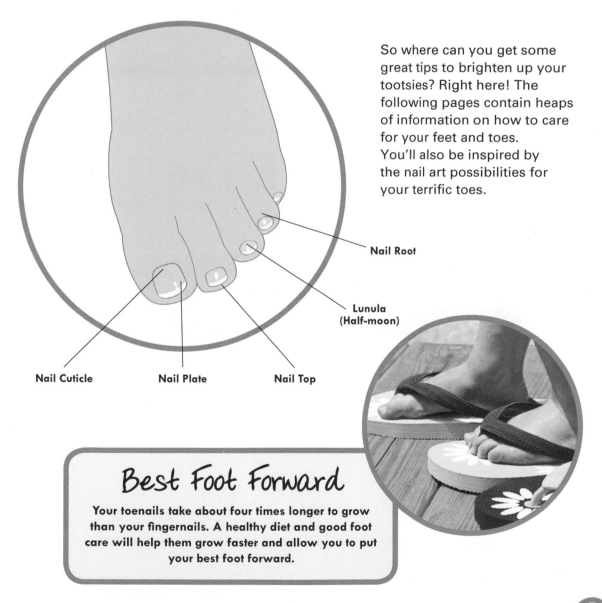

Nail Root

Lunula
(Half-moon)

Nail Cuticle   Nail Plate   Nail Top

Best Foot Forward

Your toenails take about four times longer to grow than your fingernails. A healthy diet and good foot care will help them grow faster and allow you to put your best foot forward.

Pedi Pretty

PEDICURE STEPS

Pedicures are an important step in caring for your feet and toes. They moisturise, shape and prepare your nails for the fun part of painting them or applying nail art stickers.

1 Soak your feet in a bucket of warm water for about 10 minutes.

2 Use a pumice stone to gently scrub areas of hard skin on the soles of your feet and heels.

3 Gently massage a foot scrub all over your feet to remove dead skin and give them a healthy glow. Rinse the scrub off in the bucket.

4 Use a towel to dry your feet and toes well.

5 Gently push back the cuticles (the skin around the base of the toenail) from the toenail with a cotton bud soaked in olive oil or a hoof or orange stick.

6 Buff the nail surface to remove the dull top nail cell layers.

7 Massage baby oil, olive oil or cuticle oil into the cuticle and surrounding skin of each toenail. This moisturises each cuticle thoroughly and also stimulates blood circulation in the nail bed.

8 Dry your feet thoroughly.

9 Trim your toenails to the desired length with nail scissors.

10 File your toenails into the desired shape. File from the side to the centre of the nail, holding the nail file at an angle. Never file back and forth as this may cause flaking and splitting. For a squared-off look, file nails straight across the top. For a round finish, file the nail down a little on each side and round across the top of the nail.

11 As an extra treat you can give yourself a relaxing foot massage (see pages 40 to 41).

Perfect Polish

HOW TO APPLY A SINGLE COLOUR

1 Start by buffing your toenails. This helps to prepare your nails for polish. Ideally give yourself a full pedicure before you start.

2 Place a toe separator between your toes to push them apart.

3 Apply a layer of base coat. Try to keep the base coat away from the cuticles as it has a drying effect on them. Allow to dry.

4 Apply a thin layer of your chosen nail polish colour. Paint each nail with three strokes. Start the first stroke down the centre of the nail followed by one stroke on either side of it. Allow to dry.

5 If you get any polish on the skin surrounding your toenails, dip a cotton wool bud in a little nail polish remover and remove polish carefully.

Minty Delicious

Try to get peppermint lotion foot scrubs. They smell delicious!

6 Apply a second coat of your chosen nail polish colour. Use the same technique as the first coat. It's always best to apply two coats if you can.

7 Apply a top coat to give your nails a glossy, professionally pedicured look. Allow your nails to dry, ideally for about half an hour, and then remove the toe separators. Don't put your feet into shoes for at least an hour.

Toenail Stickers

HOW TO APPLY TOENAIL STICKERS

Toenail art stickers are not permanent and are easily applied; they stick to your real nails.

1 Prepare your toenails by at least buffing them. This helps to make the nail stickers easier to stick on. Ideally follow the steps on pages 32 to 33 and give yourself a full pedicure before you begin.

2 Apply a clear nail varnish. Because your toenails produce their own natural oils, nail stickers won't stick well unless toenails are varnished.

3 Lift your chosen nail stickers from their backing sheet with tweezers.

4 Line up the nail sticker with your cuticle and place it gently on your toenail. When you are happy with the position, pat it down gently using a hoof or orange stick.

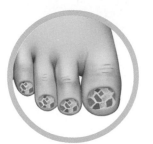

5 Trim or file the sticker as needed to fit your toenail shape.

6 Protect your toenail stickers by applying a layer of top coat.

Toenail Sticker Removal

To remove toenail stickers, wash your feet in warm soapy water and gently peel off the stickers.

Top Tip

The easiest way to get close enough to your toenails to apply toenail stickers with ease is by sitting in a chair and putting your (clean) foot on the edge of a table. Make sure there is good lighting so it's easy to see what you're doing.

Be Bold

When looking at your nail art stickers, don't feel you have to use the same design on each toe. It's fun to mix things up.

Like with your hands, not every toe needs to look the same. Your feet are further away than your hands so you can be even bolder with your toenails than you were with your fingernails. Use gems, polish, nail art stickers or, better yet, a combination of them all!

It's best to plan your toenail design creations before you start. Use the foot outlines on these pages to draw out your designs and make creative decisions before you get started.

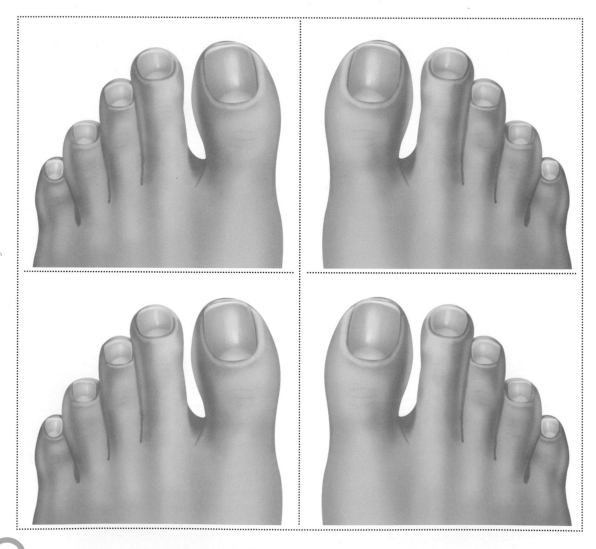

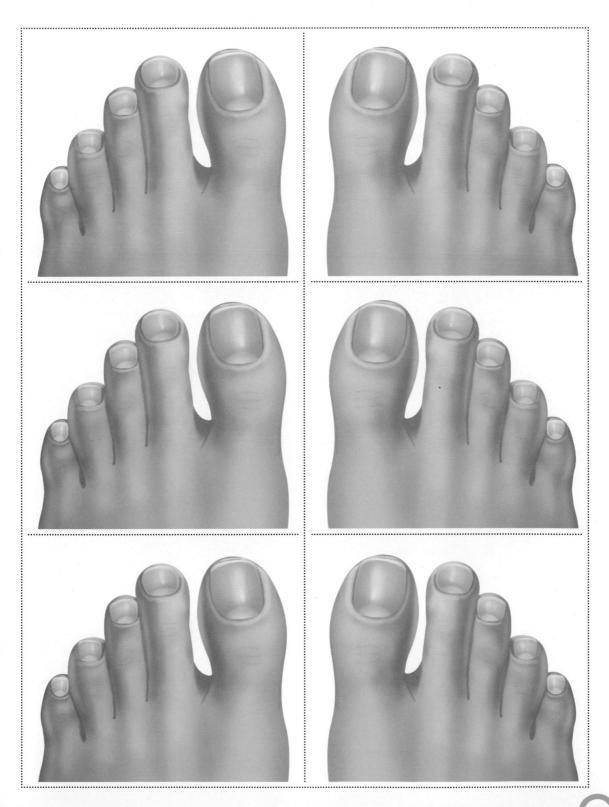

Toe Bling

HOW TO APPLY TOENAIL GEMS

Don't neglect your toes — they like to sparkle as much as your fingers.
Gems are a great way to add some bling to your toes. So let's get them twinkling.

1 Prepare your toenails by buffing them. Ideally follow the steps on pages 32 to 33 and give yourself a full pedicure before you start.

2 Apply a base coat to your toenails.

3 Choose a nail polish colour that complements the gem colours you have chosen and apply two coats. Allow to dry thoroughly.

4 Carefully peel off the protective backing from the gem.

5 Using tweezers, position the gem onto your toenail. Press firmly in place for several seconds.

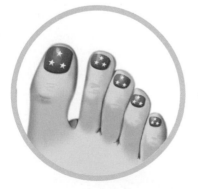

6 Apply a top coat to protect both your polish and gem.

Top Tip
You can buy nail glue from most beauty stores. Use it to re-affix any gems that fall off.

ONE OR MANY?

It's up to you whether you put one gem on each toe, five gems on your big toe or three gems on each toe. Play around and see what looks best.

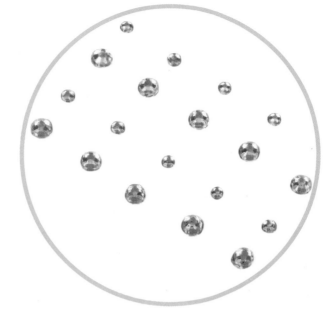

SHAPES, SIZES AND COLOURS

Gems come in different shapes, sizes and colours. It can be fun to match them to your polish colour or choose gems that contrast with your polish colour. It just depends what you're in the mood for. Think about your sandals as well and try to incorporate them into your gem choices. Silver sandals look great with silver gems.

Foot Massage

HOW TO MASSAGE YOUR FEET

Given how much you use them, sometimes your feet need the extra-special attention of a relaxing foot massage. A foot massage will improve the blood flow and relieve tired, aching muscles.

1 Sit cross-legged on the floor and place a towel under your feet to make them more comfortable.

2 Pour a little massage oil or moisturiser into the palm of your hand and rub it all over your right foot.

3 Begin the massage with your heel. Gently squeeze your heel with the palm of your hand. Repeat this four or five times.

4 Next, move to your instep. Using your thumbs, gently massage your instep from the inside of your foot up towards the ball of your foot.

5 Now focus on the ball of your foot. Gently massage the ball of your foot, stroking downwards with your thumbs, back towards your heel.

6 Move on to your toes, gently squeezing each toe four or five times.

7 Finally, massage the top of your foot, from the ankle to the toe area.

8 Wipe any excess oil or moisturiser away with a tissue.

9 Repeat on your left foot.

Top Tip

The more pressure you apply pressure you apply, the more likely you are to release tension in the muscles of the foot. If you are looking to relieve the stresses of the day, try to knead your foot deeply.

Daring Designs

Now that we have your feet healthy and smelling delicious it's time to get them looking fabulous. Toes look great painted a single colour but there's a lot more you can do. The next five pages will show you in simple steps how to create some unique toenail art designs using nail polish. Use this page to plan out your own designs.

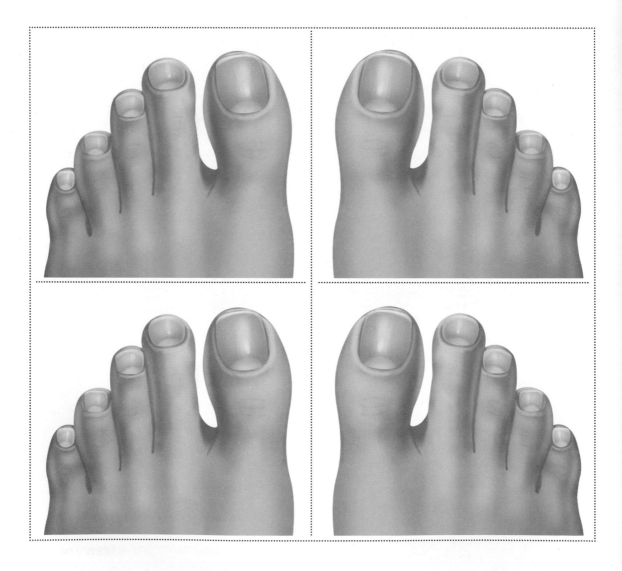

Feline Feet

HOW TO APPLY TIGER TOES

A leopard or tiger print on your toes looks really fun and striking.

1 Prepare your toenails by buffing them. Ideally follow the steps on pages 32 to 33 and give yourself a full pedicure before you start.

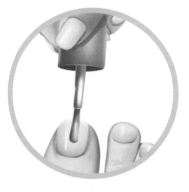

2 Follow the instructions on page 34 to apply a single colour (use a brown or yellow polish) but stop before you put on the top coat.

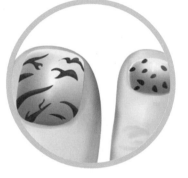

3 Use a nail art pen to draw in leopard spots or tiger stripes across your toenail with dark brown or yellow polish (choose the colour that contrasts with your base coat). If you don't have a nail art pen you can do this with the polish brush.

4 Apply a top coat to give your nails a glossy, professionally pedicured look. Allow your nails to dry for about half an hour and then remove the toe separators. Do not put your feet into shoes for at least an hour.

Top Tip

This design looks great with any gold-coloured foot jewellery, so put on any golden toe rings or anklets you have to complete this wild look.

Lightning and Stars

HOW TO APPLY LIGHTNING BOLTS AND STARS

You can incorporate the weather and nature into your nail art.
Lightning bolts make for a striking design and stars look dreamy.

1 Prepare your toenails by buffing them. Ideally follow the steps
on pages 32 to 33 and give yourself a full pedicure before you start.

2 Follow the instructions on page 34 to apply a single colour
(use a black polish) but stop before you put on the top coat.

3 Use a nail art pen to carefully paint
a bold zigzag using yellow polish down
the length of your toenail. For stars,
use a dotting tool and metallic silver polish
to apply lots of tiny dots to each toe.
Shape the dots into small stars.

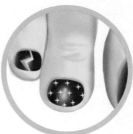

4 Apply a top coat to give your nails a glossy, professionally
pedicured look. Allow your nails to dry for about half an hour
and then remove the toe separators. Do not put your feet into
shoes for at least an hour.

Top Tip

Stars don't have to be silver and lightning
doesn't have to be yellow. Experiment
with neon colours for the boldest results.

Geometric

HOW TO APPLY GEOMETRIC DESIGNS

Sharp shapes and lines can be used to create striking nail art. With the use of tape and a steady hand it's quite easy to achieve this look.

1 Prepare your toenails by buffing them. Ideally follow the steps on pages 32 to 33 and give yourself a full pedicure before you start.

2 Follow the instructions on page 34 to apply a single colour but stop before you put on the top coat.

3 Imagine your toenail divided into four equal squares. Use sticky tape to cover three of the four squares of your toenail.

4 Using a contrasting colour to your base coat, paint the uncovered square. Once dry, apply a second coat.

5 Carefully remove the tape and move on to the next toenail.

6 Apply a top coat to give your nails a glossy, professionally pedicured look. Allow your nails to dry for about half an hour and then remove the toe separators. Do not put your feet into shoes for at least an hour.

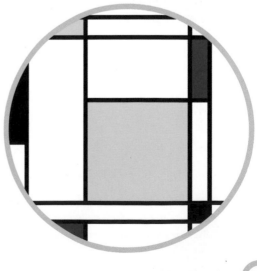

Top Tip
You don't have to cover the same square on each toe. It looks great when you mix it up.

Special Occasions

We decorate our houses for special occasions so why not our nails?
Christmas, Easter and Valentine's Day are three festive occasions that
many people celebrate and can be incorporated into our nail design.

HOW TO APPLY REINDEER TOES

1 Prepare your toenails by buffing them. Ideally follow the steps on
pages 32 to 33 and give yourself a full pedicure before you start.

2 Follow the instructions on page 34 to apply a single colour
(use white polish) but stop before you put on the top coat.

3 Apply metallic gold or dark brown polish
to the top half of your toe.

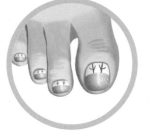

4 Use a nail art pen to draw two lines through the white polish.
Add two lines to branch off each central line and you have antlers!

5 Use black polish to add the eyes and nose (or red
polish for the nose, if you want Rudolph).

6 Apply a top coat to give your nails a glossy,
professionally pedicured look. Allow your nails
to dry for about half an hour and then remove
the toe separators. Do not put your feet into
shoes for at least an hour.

Top Tip

An easy way to make light brown polish
for the antlers is to mix dark brown polish
with some white polish.

HOW TO APPLY EASTER EGG TOES

1 Prepare your toenails by buffing them. Ideally follow the steps on pages 32 to 33 and give yourself a full pedicure before you start.

2 Follow the instructions on page 34 to apply a single colour (use a light or pastel colour polish) but stop before you put on the top coat.

3 Use a nail art pen to paint an oval egg outline. It can be hard to draw an oval shape freehand so hold your hand steady and move slowly. Decorate each egg with different colour polishes and designs.

4 Apply a top coat to give your nails a glossy, professionally pedicured look. Allow your nails to dry, ideally for about half an hour, and then remove the toe separators. Do not put your feet into shoes for at least an hour.

HOW TO APPLY LOVE HEART TOES

1 Prepare your toenails by buffing them. Ideally follow the steps on pages 32 to 33 and give yourself a full pedicure before you start.

2 Follow the instructions on page 34 to apply a single colour (use a red polish) but stop before you put on the top coat.

3 Use a nail art pen to paint and fill a love heart shape in white on each toe.

4 Apply a top coat to give your nails a glossy, professionally pedicured look. Allow your nails to dry, ideally for about half an hour, and then remove the toe separators. Do not put your feet into shoes for at least an hour.

Best Foot Forward

Creating striking and attractive nail art on your toes is so much fun. It can be tricky though, so don't give up. Take your time with it and try new things. If something doesn't work, try it again. If you really can't get it, don't worry; just move on to another design.

It's really important to keep your hand steady while attempting any nail art. You can rest it on your foot to help keep it steady and your polish smooth.

Painting your own toes can be particularly difficult, so if there is a design you just can't master, try it on someone else.

In no time you'll be able to keep your toes looking so fabulous that you'll always be able to put your best foot forward!

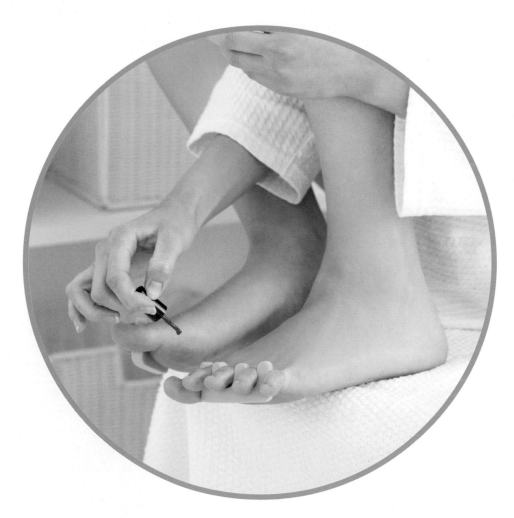